GOD TIME

GOD TIME

YOUR FIRST 31 DAYS

BRIAN WANGLER

REDEMPTION
PRESS

Published by Redemption Press, PO Box 427, Enumclaw, WA 98022 Toll Free (844) 2REDEEM (273-3336)

Redemption Press is honored to present this title in partnership with the author. The views expressed or implied in this work are those of the author. Redemption Press provides our imprint seal representing design excellence, creative content and high quality production.

ISBN 13: 978-1-63232-938-7 (Print)
　　　　 978-1-63232-939-4 (ePub)
　　　　 978-1-63232-941-7 (Mobi)

Library of Congress Catalog Card Number: 2015959688

DEDICATION

To my wife, Lindy, for all of her work in the Kingdom. For twenty-five years you have labored by my side in service to the One who redeemed us and I am grateful. Thank you Lindy for your life, your love, and three great children!

To my parents, Bill and Hilda Wangler, for instilling in me early on a passion for seeing people come to Christ. You believed and lived out the Gospel in such a way that I found my way home, and for that I am eternally grateful.

GOD TIME:
YOUR FIRST 31 DAYS

GT is a daily guide that will help you to establish a time with God in your life. It will acquaint or reacquaint you with the Word of God and introduce important biblical characters and themes that you will enjoy unpacking the rest of your life. Some basic guidelines include:

1. Select a time and place where you will daily spend fifteen to thirty minutes uninterrupted.

2. Secure a Bible, this devotional, and a pen to jot down ideas or things you need to talk to God about or that God has talked to you about.

3. Develop a process.

    a. Start **GT** by asking God to open your eyes and heart to what He wants you to know each day. Give Him the most anxious thought in your mind, perhaps the last thing you thought about last night and the first thing you thought about this morning.

    b. Use the table of contents in your Bible. Look up the Scripture for the day and read the text.

    c. Read the Scripture slowly; make notes when a particular verse or word captures your attention.

    d. Read the devotional for the day.

e. In the space provided, briefly answer the questions at the end of each day's reading.

What do I want to say to God today?

What is God saying to me today?

These brief answers are for you so don't worry about how much or how little you write or about grammar or spelling concerns. Relax. These next thirty-one days are going to be exciting! Enjoy them. Your journey has begun. May God richly bless you as you begin your new life in Christ Jesus.

Because of His mercy (Titus 3:5),

Pastor Brian

The Secret

I met God in the morning
When the day was at its best,
And His Presence came like sunrise,
Like a glory in my breast.

All day long the Presence lingered,
All day long He stayed with me,
And we sailed in perfect calmness
O'er a very troubled sea.

Other ships were blown and battered,
Other ships were sore distressed,
But the winds that seemed to drive them,
Brought to us a peace and rest.

Then I thought of other mornings,
With a keen remorse of mind,
When I too had loosed the moorings,
With the Presence left behind.

So I think I know the secret,
Learned from many a troubled way;
You must seek Him in the morning
If you want Him through the day!

—Bishop Ralph Cushman
Pocketbook of Prayer, 1941

CONTENTS

FREQUENTLY ASKED QUESTIONS

1. **What if I have trouble reading?** You are not alone! Many people struggle early in their Christian journey with reading since it may or may not be something they have done a lot of in previous years. There are other ways of getting into the Word, such as audio Bibles. Be patient; it will come. If you need help, ask your pastor or a Christian friend.

2. **What time of day should I do devotions?** There is no wrong time to do devotions. As long as you are in the Word and looking to God, anytime is the best time. The important thing is to schedule thirty minutes into your day when you will focus on your relationship with God. Some prefer morning and others evening. Choose whatever works best for you.

3. **What if I miss a day?** Pick it up the next day and go on.

4. **What if I encounter something I don't understand?** You will; we all do. That's what is so special about a local church. When you encounter a difficult question, ask a pastor, a teacher or a Christian friend for help.

5. **What else can I do to further my walk with God?** The following are four important tools a church may provide early on to assist you in the journey:

a. Sunday worship services are an important part of hearing the Word of God.

b. Becoming a part of a Sunday school class that is for people who are starting out or starting over.

c. Participation in a basic Bible study with a personal mentor has proven to be very valuable.

d. Becoming a part of a small group is also a great way to continue to walk with God as you walk with others. Accountability and help are important as we go forward.

BORN AGAIN

Read John 3:1-16.

I've only played paintball once. Our youth group was going on an outing and I was invited. We separated into two teams and the games began.

Cautious, since many of these kids had played a lot more of this game than I had, I lay down behind a log and waited on an unsuspecting adolescent "enemy" to fall into my trap. About thirty seconds into the battle, I realized there was a better place to hide just a few feet away. Carefully, I lifted my head to make sure the coast was clear when, splat, someone shot me in the face. Luckily my mask took the hit; unluckily, the game was over for me.

I wanted a do-over. What ensued was pretty pitiful: a forty-something man yelling he wants a do-over. I was quickly informed the game wasn't played that way, and they proceeded to shoot me a few more times. Finally, I begrudgingly took my seat on the sidelines to wait for the next skirmish.

There was a man named Nicodemus who came to see Jesus. He came at night because he didn't want to tarnish his reputation by being seen with the young radical who was making waves in Jerusalem. Something about Jesus made Nicodemus want to get to know Him better. What Jesus said to Nicodemus that night changed Nicodemus; it also changed the world. A world made up of people who desperately needed and wanted a do-over. The phrase "born again" was used for the first time that night.

When we accept Jesus as our Savior, we begin a process of transformation. All things become new. It is our spiritual birthday.

Happy Birthday!

A friend of mine walked into my office just a few days after accepting Christ and handed me a cigar. With a smile on his face he said, "I've been born again and I've decided to celebrate." I thanked him and placed the cigar in my desk drawer. He returned a few weeks later to apologize. Sheepishly, he said, "I didn't realize Nazarene pastors aren't supposed to smoke." I told him I hadn't smoked it, but wanted to keep it. He agreed to let me keep it if I promised not to smoke it. We laughed together celebrating his new life all over again.

I kept the cigar for a long time, but somewhere in a move I lost it. I regret losing it. Every time I opened my desk drawer and smelled the cigar, I was reminded of the amazing transformation God does in all of us. God is good. And by the way, *Happy Birthday!* Enjoy!

What do I want to say to God today?

What is God saying to me today?

Read Luke 15:1-31.

Like the combination on a padlock, the numbers **15-?-3** open up a great treasure. The reading comes from Luke **15**. There are **31** verses. There are **3** stories. There is one overriding, all-important message locked inside. In these early stages of your journey, become acquainted with the great stories of the Bible. Jesus is a great storyteller and each story he told is bursting with wisdom for your life.

Luke 15:1-7. A sheep has wandered away from the flock and from the shepherd. That spells trouble for the sheep and heartbreak for the shepherd. There are 100 sheep and only one is missing, but the Shepherd can't live with that math so He leaves the 99 and goes off in search of the one. He risks everything for the sake of one. That kind of decision-making might make for a poor rancher, but it makes for a great shepherd. When Jesus finds the sheep, He brings it home and the celebration begins.

Luke15:8-10. A woman has lost a coin. She has nine other coins but refuses to give up on the one that is missing. She searches. And she searches. She lights a lamp and sweeps the house clean. She searches until she finds the coin and then the celebration begins.

Luke 15:11-31. An ungrateful son demands an early inheritance from his father so he can live the high life. The demand speaks clearly about how the son feels about the father; he wishes he were dead. The father's response ... espect he has for his son; he gives him what he asks ... go. The son leaves home with no intention of return, and ... thought of the broken hearts he leaves behind. Difficul... big wide world with one goal: pleasure. The son ... off ... enjoys it. He then discovers that what he He ... is ... buying to own, he was only renting. When the thought ... was p... money runs out, ... shame creeps in. One day he finds himself broke and broken, one and in agony. But then a miracle happens. He comes to his senses. He imagines how better life would be if he were just an employee of the man who used to call him son. He wonders if there's any way to go home. He rehearses his confession speech. He won't ask for acceptance back into the family; he'll just beg for scraps from the table. He waits and he hopes and he trembles at the thought of the wrath that is to come. Still, he goes home because he has nowhere else to go.

Finally he sees home in the distance. He spots familiar landmarks and knows he is almost there. The hill he used to play on, the neighbors he used to know, the trees he used to climb, all surround him as he looks down the street that used to lead home. And then he sees something else: a familiar figure, and tear-stained face, a man running toward him; his father. The son confesses, the father weeps, and celebration ensues.

So, what point is Jesus making? The message is this: He's glad you're here. You're far more valuable than you realize. Your Father has spared no expense to find you and will withhold nothing from you. Jesus Christ called all of heaven to rejoice the day you came home. He was waiting for you before you were looking for Him. It's called grace. It is unconditional; it is unparalleled; it is unbelievable; it is the most powerful force on earth. And, my friend, it is yours. Welcome home! Enjoy.

What do I want to say to God today?

What is God saying to me today?

GOT QUESTIONS?

Read Matthew 4:18-22.

What does it mean to be a Christian? Am I a Christian? What do I do? What do I say? Do I need to choose different friends? Why is everyone here so friendly? Why is everyone here so judgmental? What about all the wrongs I've done? Is there something I need to do to correct them? Where do I start? How am I supposed to pray? Where am I supposed to pray? For that matter, why am I supposed to pray? What if I fail? What if this new experience is just some emotional high? What if I don't feel anything? Why don't I feel something? What do I need to get rid of? What do I need to keep? Are these shorts too short? When can I sing in the praise team? Why didn't pastor speak to me today? What if this whole thing is a cult? Where is the book of Daniel? Why is the Bible so hard to understand? Where did the Bible come from? Who cares about who "begot" whom? What version of the Bible should I read? Why does the pastor preach so long? Why is the music so loud, or soft, or whatever? Can I stay at home and watch television on Sunday and worship God that way? What is worship anyway? Am I good to go on the heaven thing? If I slip up do I lose my salvation? Should I be baptized? Did the fact that I was baptized as a baby count? If I sin, do I have to start all over? How do I do that?

Have questions? That's okay; everyone does. Just remember the key to being a Christian is following Jesus. Jesus came to where Peter was, just as He came to where you were. Jesus spoke personally to Peter, just like He did to you. Peter responded, just like you did. Jesus asked Peter to follow Him; that is all Jesus asks of you.

Jesus said He would make Peter into something and He did. Jesus will do the same for you. Being a Christian is about following Jesus. He will lead and guide. All you have to do is follow. There will be things to let go of, things to do and not do, and everything in between, but the key is following Jesus. Relax. It's a lifelong journey. He's a great God. And you are on the right road! Enjoy.

What do I want to say to God today?

What is God is saying to me today?

YOUR BIBLE

Read Hebrews 4:12-13.

The Bible can be intimidating. It is, however, the most powerful tool that God gives us as we seek to follow Him. This devotional will introduce you to some key Scriptures and characters. Your Bible is not like other books:

- It is living. The Bible has the ability to speak to you exactly where you are.
- It is active. The Bible will call you to action and search your heart. It penetrates and reveals the difference between what you feel, what you think, and what God is saying to you. It gets inside your actions to discover your motives. It will penetrate your heart and keep you from sin.
- It judges. The Bible, applied to our lives by the Holy Spirit, is the final authority in the life of believers.

Use your Bible as a tool. Don't be afraid to mark in it and make it yours. Take it with you and look for moments during the day when you can spend time with God. Set aside a specific time each day to be alone with Him. Ask God to direct you as you open up His Word. Use your Bible when you listen to sermons. Jot down questions and seek answers from your pastor, teacher, or mentor. Take time to memorize key verses of Scripture like (John 3:16; Matthew 28:19-20; Proverbs 3:5-6; Matthew 22:37-39). The Word of God is the fully-inspired message from your Creator to you. Are you ready to get started on an incredible journey? A good place to begin is the book of John. Enjoy.

Read the Bible completely like a love letter; consult it constantly like a road map; study it carefully like a lesson book; and obey it conscientiously like an army order.

—Roy Zuck

What do I want to say to God today?

What is God saying to me today?

WHAT JUST HAPPENED TO ME? *FORGIVEN*

Read 1 John 1:9 and Psalm 103:11-12.

Years ago I worked for a financial services company that dealt with retirement accounts. Much of the work involved moving money from one investment to another. An issue requiring special care was protecting accounts from tax liability in the transfer.

I remember a particularly painful incident when I was young and in a hurry. Fred, a medical doctor, made his first (very large) investment with me. That's the good news. The bad news is I made a mistake in the transfer and Fred got a tax bill. When the company received notice of what had happened, my boss made it very clear I was to immediately notify Fred of the mistake and "make it right."

I drove to Fred's house that night wondering how I was ever going to make it right. What had my boss meant by that? Even if the law allowed it, I certainly didn't have the money to pay the bill. I was in major trouble.

I parked my car and walked up to his house. Fred greeted me at the door. We sat down and I got right to the point. I don't remember everything I said, but I remember closing with the words, "I am very, very, sorry, sir."

Fred shuffled the papers a bit, laid them on the table, and sat back in his chair. He then began to share his life story. He related how hard his life had been but how God had always provided. Fred concluded by saying, "Since God has been so good to me, Brian, I try not to focus on the mistakes of others. The mistake is forgiven. Let's move on." With that, he stood and asked, "Have I ever shown you my piano?"

It would be several years after my encounter with Fred before I would become a Christian. As my pastor began to explain how God forgives us when we ask Him, I thought about my experience with Fred. I can almost hear the piano playing. God loves you, my friend, and you have been forgiven. Enjoy.

What do I want to say to God today?

What is God saying to me today?

WHAT JUST HAPPENED TO ME?
ALIVE

Read Ephesians 2:1-10.

The biblical term, *regeneration*, is used when describing the new life that is ours when we become a Christian. Regeneration means we are remade spiritually—we are "born again." Regeneration also changes how we view God, the world, and everyone and everything in it.

I still remember the day I first got glasses. I was in my early twenties and was unaware I had a problem until I heard my friends talking about a sign on the wall of the bowling alley. When I realized I couldn't see what they were seeing, I decided I better go for a checkup.

After tests, measurements, and a prescription for glasses, I was on my way. Wow! What a difference. I couldn't get over how different everything looked. Colors seemed brighter. I could see each leaf on the trees and each brick on the buildings. It was amazing; it was like I was seeing things for the first time.

The doctor laughed when I told him how incredible everything looked. He said, "Mr. Wangler, you're going to make a lot of other drivers very happy, too!"

Not everyone experiences the same feelings or emotions during the first few days of following Jesus, but everyone *is* changed. We begin to see things differently, including ourselves. It can be very discouraging after we have become a Christian to see we still struggle with sin. We wonder, "Did I really get saved?" The answer to that question can be found in the *struggle*. The truth is, before we were saved, we didn't struggle with sin; we just sinned. But now, as new believers, we may still sin, but it's not okay anymore. It bothers us now.

Don't be discouraged if you're not yet where you want to be. Instead be encouraged that you're renewed and alive! And know that God will continue to renew you in the days to come. He will give you a life that is full and free; a new life in Christ Jesus! Enjoy.

What do I want to say to God today?

What is God saying to me today?

WHAT JUST HAPPENED TO ME? *JUSTIFIED*

Read Romans 3:21-26.

"Just-as-if-you never sinned"

Webster defines *justify* as 1) "to be shown to be just (right or fair); 2) to be free from blame." In biblical terms this means God has met all the requirements of His holy law by providing the sinless Son of God as the atoning sacrifice for your sins. When you received Christ as your Savior you were justified. You owed a debt you could not pay. Jesus paid your bill in your place. Now, not only is the debt erased, but you are treated as if it never existed. That's how powerful the blood of Jesus is when applied to someone's life. The Bible says it goes so far as to cleanse even the stain of sin (Ephesians 5:27).

When my children were little I wanted them to experience having a real Christmas tree. We put the tree in a holder on an old rug so water wouldn't get on the new carpet. We really enjoyed our live Christmas tree; especially the way it smelled.

After a few days, something began to change; the aroma was somehow different. Did I mention we had a cat? Apparently there is something about a real tree that affects a cat's bladder. Did I mention the old rug was bright red? Did I mention the new carpet was cream colored? The stain left on the carpet looked as if a murder had occurred—which is what I wanted to do to the cat. What a mess. What a stain.

We dabbed, we shampooed, we scrubbed, and we tried home remedies, store remedies, and everything in between. Nothing worked. The bright red stain was there to stay.

I thought about this incident the other day as I typed the word "justified" into my computer dictionary. To be "justified" is one of the things that happen when we accept Christ. We are "justified" before God and our sin is of no consequence to Him.

There are earthly consequences for sin. If you've committed a crime, you may still have to "do the time." As a matter of fact, I did have to forfeit some of my security deposit when we moved.

However, when we are justified by God's grace, the stain of sin is removed forever. The eternal consequence is gone. You are not stained. You are clean. You are His. You are justified. Celebrate His gift of justification today! Enjoy.

What do I want to say to God today?

What is God saying to me today?

WHAT JUST HAPPENED TO ME? *ADOPTED*

Read Romans 8:15-17.

We have briefly looked at three things that happened to you when you accepted Jesus Christ as your Savior: forgiveness, regeneration, and justification. Now let's look at the fourth: adoption. As a new believer, you have been adopted into the family of God.

There's nothing quite like family when it's working the way God intended. People who know you best, and love you the most. Humans, prone to chaos and calamity, but committed to seeing life through because that's what families are designed to do; see life through. To be family, is to be welcome. To be family, is to be at ease. To be family, is to never be alone.

Once there was a little girl in China who did not have a family or home. She was an orphan. A couple decided to adopt her. Adoption is an unbelievably long, tedious, and expensive process. The couple had to travel a long way to get her. The journey was not easy; there were even dangers along the way. Still they went; determined not to return without her. On the first Sunday after their return, they came to church with beaming faces tenderly cradling their precious cargo. They had adopted Sara.

Sara's life had changed. She would soon be a citizen of the United States of America. She now had a home, a future, a provider, someone to hold her, and someone to protect her. Sara had a family.

Our life is very similar to Sara's. We were once without a spiritual family, but because of what Jesus did, we can be adopted into His family. God was determined we would be His "heirs." Jesus was willing to pay an awful price for your adoption. He made the long journey from heaven to where you were. He faced many dangers along the way. He never once considered anything but bringing you home. The Bible teaches us Jesus is not ashamed to "call us brothers." That's just the kind of God He is. Enjoy.

What do I want to say to God today?

What is God saying to me today?

THE PLAN

Read Jeremiah 29:11-13.

I am an American male. I hate instructions. I don't need directions. I'd much rather just figure it out. It's not that I won't make mistakes; that's why there is duct tape. Please don't make me read directions. I confess: I have walked into a gas station pretending to ask directions and then returned to the car and said, "That guy doesn't have a clue!" I then speed away fast because that's what you do when you're lost—go nowhere fast.

Jeremiah is often referred to as the "weeping prophet." Even though he tried to warn the people the direction they were headed was wrong, they kept going that way anyway. Finally their sins came back on them and a foreign people conquered them. Everything they knew was destroyed and gone. Everything, that is, except their God. He did not abandon them even though they had abandoned Him. Although, because of their disobedience they faced a very difficult situation, God's promise was that He still had a plan for them.

In those times when life seems hopeless, remember, God has a plan. In the midst of confusion, He still has a plan. Regardless of the scoreboard, He still has a plan. No matter how many times or how seriously you have blown it, God still has plan. You may not know the plan, but God does.

Your quest needs to be one of seeking Him instead of seeking answers. He is the Plan. Jesus referred to himself as the "Way" (John 14:6). Your task is to seek Him with all of your heart. His promise is you will "find" when you do. There is an old story about a railroad engineer who asked his pastor, "Preacher, do you think the engineer is still on this train?" The answer is "Yes!" Begin to seek Him today; He has a plan for you. Enjoy.

THE PLAN

What do I want to say to God today?

What is God saying to me today?

FROM NOW ON

Read Luke 5:1-11.

Real life change is difficult and elusive. Most Americans have closets full of clothing designed for athletic participation that are being used primarily for athletic observation. This truth is illustrated by the fact that we are the best-dressed couch potatoes in the world.

To become different is not simply to act, or dress, or talk different. True change is an inside job. In today's Scripture reading, Christ did not ask Simon to change and then follow him; He asked him to follow Him so He could help Simon become what he was intended to become. Simon was still Simon; he would have human struggles and limitations. Simon was still Simon. We need to understand that; Simon did.

Just like us, Simon's faith journey included moments of growth through crisis and process. And like us, Simon had a long way to go to become what Jesus wanted him to be. In both cases, the journey begins with a first step. If you've asked Christ to forgive you of your sins and, like Simon, set out to follow Him, then these changes have already begun in you. What are those unique changes that both you and Simon share?

The **direction** is different. Simon has chosen to follow Christ. Simon chose to go travel with Christ and not run with a crowd of people who are happy to run in circles. What a difference that makes!

The **desire** is different. Simon has been forgiven. He confesses sin; he wants to be clean. Acknowledging before Jesus that he is a "sinful man" liberates him from the bondage of pride and opens the way for Jesus to welcome him into a new family.

The **destiny** is different. Now he can become what he was intended to become. Jesus said, "Don't be afraid." Imagine and embrace a life without fear because of whom and whose you are! Remember, you have a destiny and that destiny is in Christ. Simon's *spiritual* **DNA** is different. Simon is alive spiritually. He is now talking and walking with God! Thank God for what you are becoming in Him! Enjoy.

What do I want to say to God today?

What is God saying to me today?

INVITED

Read Matthew 5:1-10; 2 Timothy 3:14-17.

I marvel at the fact that relationship with God is possible. Think about it; the eternal God, the Creator God, wants to have a personal relationship with you.

The first passage of Scripture you read today is called the Beatitudes. Jesus shared these teachings with His disciples one day long ago. Jesus wants to share these teachings with you, His newest disciple, today.

I love to think of Jesus unhurriedly walking out onto a hillside and sitting down to talk with his followers. The topic for the day: "blessedness" or "happiness." The teacher: Jesus. There were surprises that day. Jesus taught that happiness is not always where we think it should be. It would have been amazing to be there. Well, guess what? As a Christian, you *are* there. Any time you open the Word of God and seek to hear from God, you are there. And Jesus is still teaching. The Bible is not like other books; it is "living and active" (Hebrews 4:12).

That's why having time alone with God and the Bible is so important. These moments are your moments and His moments. The daily discipline of getting into His presence will be essential to your spiritual growth. It is the time you are alone with the creator of the universe, the one who forgave your sins and died on the cross in your place. Guard these moments carefully. Treasure them and they will bring you rewards beyond measure.

Remember, these moments are about growing in your relationship with God. Make the time intentional and unhurried.

These are the moments that will change and transform your life. What are you doing to make sure you have time with God every day? Enjoy.

What do I want to say to God today?

What is God saying to me today?

CHURCH: WHY?

Read Matthew 16:13-20 and Hebrews 10:19-25.

The Church was God's Idea!

If you ever wondered if God has a sense of humor, getting to know His people will remove any doubt. I love the church. I've seen all sides of it and I still love it.

One thing we know, "Christ loved the church and gave himself up for her" (Ephesians 5:25). When he was illustrating the love a husband should have for his wife, Paul used the example of the love Christ had for the church. That's how much Jesus loved the church.

When I was a kid I went to church because I had to. As a young adult the only reason I went to church was to please my parents. I'd go on Mother's Day, Father's Day, Easter, Christmas; that sort of thing. It's not that I had rejected a belief in God; it's just that I hadn't really confirmed it either.

Thankfully, over the years the church never let me fully disconnect. People continued to pray for me even though I wasn't there. Every few months I'd get a phone call or a visit from someone who had watched me grow up in the church and was concerned about the direction I was going. That's just the way the church should be.

Now I go to church for a lot of reasons. There are people there I love and who love me. There are people whose lives are examples of God's amazing grace and I want my children to know them. I am encouraged and challenged by the church. I go to church because I want to honor God. But mostly I go to church because God meets me there; sometimes in the music, often through the teaching, occasionally through the smile of a friend, and always in His Word. Yes, God meets me there.

I've often heard the excuse that goes something like: "Just because you go to church doesn't make you a Christian." That's true—to a point. It's true that going to church doesn't make you a Christian any more than being in the water makes you a fish. But where do you find fish? Think about it. Enjoy.

What do I want to say to God today?

What is God saying to me today?

THE GREATEST RESCUE MISSION OF ALL TIME

Read Luke 19:1-10.

Two of the most frequently asked questions people have are about the purpose of the local church. What is the church for? What is it supposed to do?

Churches provide a place and atmosphere for worship. They help hurting people, feed the hungry, and clothe the homeless. They provide a place where Christians can support and encourage each other. Some churches take on social and political issues and fight for moral issues like human life and human rights. Some churches support and send missionaries around the world; some churches minister to the people on their block. Churches teach children and adults about God. Churches preach a message of salvation to people who are facing eternity without God.

There's a lot of talk these days about purpose and mission. Companies have mission statements and millions of books are sold to help individuals discover their personal mission statement. So what does God want to do with your church, here and now?

The best place to start is with the Scripture you just read. Jesus certainly had a purpose and mission. Shouldn't Christ's mission be our mission? If so, then the local church should be about "seeking and saving that which was lost"—whatever that looks like.

That mission and purpose will require an army. The church is that army.

Since it is apparent to everyone that the church isn't perfect because it's made up of people, some people refer to the church as a hospital because we're all sick and in need of help. Okay, but that makes for kind of a feeble army, doesn't it? The truth is, we all have been impacted with the sickness of sin, but that sickness need no longer define us; our Captain does. I prefer the idea of the body of Christ as a battleship. It's true we have our sick bay, and all of us will go there to recover once in a while, but we are much more than that. We are a people called, armed, and equipped to carry out the greatest rescue mission of all time. Are you onboard? Enjoy.

What do I want to say to God today?

What is God saying to me today?

BLESSED, BROKEN, AND GIVEN AWAY

Read Matthew 26:26-30 and 1 Corinthians 11:23-26.

One of the first vacation memories I have as a child is visiting the Alamo in San Antonio, Texas. It was in this building of rock, stone, and clay that 187 men took their stand against more than 3,000 Mexican soldiers under the leadership of General Antonio Lopez de Santa Anna. The year was 1836, and for the 187, it was a battle for freedom. Santa Anna sent a message to the commanding officer, Col. Travis, demanding surrender. Travis responded by firing a cannon. There was no way Travis would defeat the large army he was facing, but there was no way he would surrender the Alamo. The cost of surrender was too high. The 187 fell, and Santa Anna temporarily claimed victory.

Some mighty warriors died at the Alamo: Davey Crockett, Jim Bowie, and Col. William Barrett Travis. However, it is the bravery and courage exhibited by the 187 that has lived long after the battle. Their memories became battle cries when just two months after the fall of the Alamo, an army of Texans under the leadership of Sam Houston routed Santa Anna's army shouting, "Remember the Alamo!" Ask some Texans and they'll tell you the story.

Ask some Christians and they'll tell you another story about another battle and another battle cry. It's about a Savior who came to liberate people who were in bondage and destined to die until Jesus set them free. On the night that He was betrayed, Jesus initiated a sacrament we still honor today. He wanted his followers to remember something very important. While they were eating, He took the bread, blessed it, broke it, and then He gave it to the disciples.

Blessed, broken, and given away. That's the way Jesus wanted to be remembered and the way He wants us to live. Holy Communion is special. It is remembering and honoring our Savior and committing to His cause. It's remembering our sins have been forgiven, our hearts have been washed, and our lives have been redeemed. It's remembering that in your darkest hour Jesus refused to surrender you to the enemy. It is returning to the scene of our salvation, the cross, to humble ourselves as a grateful people, set free. It is a reminder that another banquet awaits us in heaven at our journey's end.

Communion has come to mean very different things to people over the 2,000 years since Christ's death and resurrection. One thing is sure—Jesus meets us there. Let's pick up the battle cry of the apostle Paul and, "Remember Jesus Christ, raised from the dead, descended from David" (2 Timothy 2:8). Celebrate His presence! Enjoy.

What do I want to say to God today?

What is God saying to me today?

BAPTISM

"Why shouldn't I?"

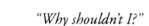

Read Matthew 3:13-17, 28:16-20, and Acts 8:26-39.

Jesus gave us two sacraments: two things He wanted us to do to remember our salvation and His sacrifice. One is communion and the other is baptism. I believe the reason He kept the list short was He knew if He didn't, we'd pay more attention to the rituals than we would to Him. The key to being a Christ follower is our relationship with Him, not ritual. Baptism is one of the rituals Jesus still calls us to practice today.

The symbolism of baptism is simple. The water represents the death we die to self, the cleansing we have in Christ, and the newness of life we have as we emerge from the water. Some people believe there's only one way to be baptized and that is submersion, meaning you stand in a baptistery or an outdoor body of water and the preacher dunks you in the name of the Father, Son, and Holy Ghost. Others think that as long as the heart is right and the water is wet it doesn't matter if you're sprinkled or squirted or dunked; you've been baptized. I agree with the latter, but always prefer dunking just because the symbolism of going under and coming up is so powerful. Whichever way you choose, as a Christian it is important you be baptized. It is also important to remember Christians get baptized because they are Christians, not in order to become one.

Still, there is something wonderful about baptism that goes beyond the fact it is a testimony to our friends and family about what Christ has done in our lives. God always meets us in moments of obedience, and baptism is no exception. When Jesus was baptized, the Bible says the Holy Spirit descended like a dove and lighted on Jesus. I've never seen a dove descend during baptism, but sometimes the Holy Spirit shows up in other ways.

Michelle was twenty-something when she told me that even though she'd grown up in the church, she had never been baptized. Through tears, she told me, "It's time." I'll never forget the mental image I have of Michelle's face when she came up out of the water. She wept, we cheered, and her smile told the story. God met Michelle in the baptismal waters.

Gene was well into his seventies when he accepted Christ. Gene was an encourager. When Gene came up out of the water, he gave me a hug I'll never forget. Gene started telling people Jesus loved them while he was still in the water and hasn't stopped since. God met Gene in the waters of baptism.

Ray was close to eighty when he accepted Christ and asked to be baptized. I watched as his son, Steve, one of our staff pastors, baptized his father. Ray was quick to talk about the Lord and quicker to serve Him. He became one of our greeters and though his health began to fail relatively soon after he accepted Christ, Ray served Him to the end.

The faces and names from nearly twenty years of experiencing the baptismal waters are many. The testimony is the same: God meets people there. I've baptized people in backyard swimming pools, farm ponds, and indoor church baptisteries. The locations change, but God's presence is always there.

In the first text you just read, Jesus is baptized. In the second, Jesus commanded all believers to be baptized, and in the third, an Ethiopian eunuch asks, "Why shouldn't I be baptized?" So why shouldn't *you*?

Enjoy.

BAPTISM

What do I want to say to God today?

What is God saying to me today?

OVERHAUL

Read 2 Corinthians 5:17.

I once had a car that was a challenge to get started and a "your-guess-is-as-good-as-mine" for how long it would stay that way. I did what I could to keep it going, but it was difficult because there always seemed to be something wrong. I changed the oil; actually, I just kept adding oil. I changed the spark plugs, filters, and hoses. The battery went bad so I replaced it, which revealed the starter was bad. I even became comfortable using mechanic type phrases; words like timing and transmission.

I talked to people who were familiar with car problems. They'd say, "You probably just need a tune-up," or, "Your timing may be off," or, "New spark plugs will make her hum like a baby." I would always nod like I knew what they were talking about and then wonder what humming had to do with car repair.

Ultimately, I had to go to a mechanic. As the mechanic opened the hood, I mentioned, "She (guys call cars "she") may need a tune up." He mentioned it would be best if I went to the waiting area.

After what seemed like hours, he came to get me, "Mr. Wangler, you don't need a tune-up." What a relief! I was thinking a tune-up would be about $150. "What you need is a complete overhaul. It will cost $1,200." Reluctantly, I turned over the car keys and approved the work.

When I picked up the car, she was awesome. She now hummed like a baby. I no longer had to park on an incline in case it wouldn't start. I was thinking about us, about you and me and everyone else driving down life's highway. There comes a time when quick fixes or a tune-ups don't fix us—what we need is a complete overhaul. That's what God does when we stop trying to be our own mechanics. Oh, you'll still have some dents and rust on the outside, but over time Jesus changes us from the inside out.

Everything in life changes when Jesus is Lord. It may take a while for you to feel it, and even longer for you to see it, but if you have given Him the keys, He's ready to work. Are you ready? Enjoy.

What do I want to say to God today?

What is God saying to me today?

WHO STARTED THIS?

Read Philippians 1:3-6.

One thing that is good to remember every once in a while is the fact your journey did not start with you but with the One who made you—God. We come to Christ because God has drawn us to Him. Your journey was His idea, not yours. Your response was necessary to begin the journey, as it will be necessary to continue the journey, but it is God's idea that you get saved. What a great place to be!

If your salvation is His idea, then He knew what your struggles would be. He's God. If your salvation was His idea, then He's not surprised when you stumble. Your failure may surprise you, but it won't Him. He's God. He knew your weaknesses when He called you. He's God. If He is the one who started His work in your life, then you can be sure He will be the One to finish it.

Some time ago I was asked to officiate at a renewal-of-vows wedding ceremony. The couple had been married fifty years. They had raised five children and weathered the many storms of life that come with a fifty-year journey. They wept as they repeated their vows. Then they kissed, and kissed, and kissed! People began to giggle.

Finally, someone in the crowd whistled and yelled, "I was at your first wedding and you didn't kiss her that long!"

The couple laughed and eventually stopped kissing. Then the groom responded to the heckler, "The real surprise is she's still willing to kiss me back after all these years."

It's one thing to stand at an altar, young and full of passion to commit to love someone unconditionally. It's quite another to stand at an altar, older and full of life experiences, and commit to the same person, again. This time around she knows his faults and he knows hers.

I was thinking about God and how He loved us, died for us, and chose us even when He already knew all of our faults. He knew we would stumble. He knew we would fail. He knew we would get angry. He knew He would have to rescue us time after time, but He did it anyway. That's just the kind of God He is. Thank God for His faithfulness to draw you to Christ, and remember: God always finishes what He starts! Enjoy.

WHO STARTED THIS?

What do I want to say to God today?

What is God saying to me today?

MYSTERIES

Read Proverbs 16:11 and 1 Corinthians 13:12.

I remember as a teenager hearing a sermon about the mysteries of life. The speaker said, "There are three things that must be surrendered to the Lord if you're going to serve God: your money, your marriage, and your mysteries."

Consider the mysteries. Proverbs 16:11 reminds me that, at the end of the day, God owes me no explanation. What is fair and right are for Him to decide. He holds all the weights and measures in His bag. Fairness is for Him to decide.

That's a hard pill to swallow when bad things happen to good people. From one end of the suffering spectrum to the other, there is one question that persists: "Why?" Some of the most ignorant and foolish comments I've heard made were by people who were trying to explain the reason something bad happened.

For instance, standing by a father who had lost his teenage son in a drowning accident, I listened as person after person, well meaning I'm sure, looked into his eyes and tried to explain. Some said, "Well, I guess God needed another angel!" Others speculated on what they thought God needed when He took the boy. One even mentioned, "Maybe God needs a first baseman." My friend was more gracious than I was about the comments. He just smiled and said, "Thank you." Graciousness shows up in some pretty unexpected faces sometimes.

It lived in his. Still, when the funeral was over and the crowd left, my friend sat contemplating what had just happened.

He knew the details. His son, Troy, along with two other boys had slipped down to a local swimming hole in the Vermilion River. One of the boys got caught in the undercurrent and began to scream for help. Troy jumped in to save him. As Troy swam toward him, the first boy kicked free of the current. The boy escaped; his rescuer, Troy, did not. Almost as if it had negotiated a trade, the current cut the first young man loose but took Troy. They recovered his body seven hours later downstream. And the questions began. What my friend, Dan, struggled with was not what had happened, but why.

After a few months he called and we met for coffee. He seemed better, not well, but better. "I've decided something," he said stirring his coffee. "I've decided to trust God with what happened." Now it was my turn to ask the questions. "Why?" I asked. "Why and how do you do that?"

Dan smiled and shifted in his seat, took a drink of coffee and responded. "Late one night I was arguing with God. I guess we weren't really arguing, I was just yelling at Him. I wanted to know why. It was funny," Dan said, "but He answered my question with a question. I felt like God was saying to me, *Dan, as sad as what's happened is, would there be any possible outcome to Troy's life that would be worse?*

Dan wiped a tear away and continued. "I had to be honest, Brian. Of course, there could be worse endings to Troy's life. Troy was a Christian, for one thing. Troy died a hero, for another. Troy didn't suffer, Troy didn't waste away, and Troy will always be remembered for his courage and faith. When I began to make the list, I began to understand what God was getting at." I sat back and continued listening. Dan leaned forward and spoke, "That's why I have actually been able to say 'Thank you' to God for taking care of Troy. Troy belonged to Him and He knew what was best."

My friend Dan went on to live out that kind of trust in God for the rest of his life. He had serious health issues and family and personal issues plagued him, but Dan never lost his faith. Where others grew bitter, Dan grew better and never lost his smile. The last time I visited him in the hospital, diabetes had taken his sight and was about to take his life even though he was still a young man. Still, Dan smiled.

We visited for a few moments and then prayed together. Finally, I turned to leave. As I reached the door, Dan called my name and I turned. He sat up in his bed as much as he could, smiled, and said, "Brian, I love you. You've been a good friend." I walked back over, and we embraced and cried. A few days later Dan was gone. He was in heaven and the mystery, at least from Dan's perspective, was solved. (See 1 Corinthians 13:12.) God can be trusted with your mysteries, and life is far too short to play the victim. He holds the weights and measures and mysteries. Trust Him! Enjoy.

What do I want to say to God today?

What is God saying to me today?

DANIEL'S DECISION

Read Daniel 1:1-17.

The armies of Nebuchadnezzar of Babylonia surrounded the city of Jerusalem and utterly destroyed and defeated it. That day everything in Daniel's life changed. This young, handsome, intelligent, Hebrew boy was deliberately separated from his parents and carried into captivity. As he was chained and led away from the only life he'd ever known, Daniel must surely have asked, "Why?"

Why? The Hebrew nation and its leaders had repeatedly ignored God's direction and broken their covenant with Him. It's a terrible moment when our sin and the consequences of that sin come crashing down. What do you do when everything seems to fall apart? What do you do when it seems as if you have no control over what's happening? To whom do you look?

First, know that as a child of God you always have options. Daniel was separated from his people that day, but not from his God. This realization sets the stage for everything else that happens in Daniel's life. Daniel held fast to the fact that people, not God, had failed him. Daniel made a decision, a commitment, and a choice to honor God, even in the adversity of captivity.

The king ordered a group of young men be selected to be groomed for service in the king's palace. Instead of slavery, they would be trained in the language and literature of the Babylonians, educated by the finest teachers, and fed at the king's table. And there is the rub.

As a Hebrew, Daniel had been taught to observe very strict food laws. The food at the king's table was in violation of God's law. To refuse to eat the food could easily end in death. "But Daniel resolved . . ." and "purposed in his heart." Consequently, Daniel refused the offer of the king.

The rest of Daniel's story is the kind of adventure movies are made of as God honors his decision, spares Daniel and his three friends' lives, and blesses them in ways that defy explanation.

"To these four young men God gave . . ." Daniel had found the key to life: total, absolute obedience to God. Thousands of years have not changed the key. Regardless of the circumstances, we must make a choice: Whom will I trust? Whom will I follow? How will I purpose my heart? Determine today to trust God. Determine today to purpose your heart toward God. Determine today that even when things seem out of your control, you will choose to obey God. And God will determine the glory of your destiny. Enjoy the journey.

What do I want to say to God today?

What is God saying to me today?

NEHEMIAH—EVERY
HEART HAS A CALL!

Read Nehemiah 1:1-11 and 2:12.

The book of Nehemiah tells the story about a man discovering God's purpose for his life. Nehemiah was carried into captivity when Jerusalem fell. He had been chosen to be the king's cupbearer, a very trusted, honored, and essential position.

One day he received word that things were not going well back in Jerusalem. The Jewish remnant was trying to rebuild the city. What follows this troubling news is an amazing story of how God worked in the lives of the Jewish people as Nehemiah becomes the leader who helps to rebuild the walls of Jerusalem in just fifty-two days.

The success of this great accomplishment is found in Nehemiah 2:12, "What my God had put in my heart." Nehemiah was not acting on an emotion, but on a *purpose* God had placed in his heart. It's that God *purpose* each of us needs to discover and follow.

The way Nehemiah discovered his purpose is a lot like the way we discover ours. Nehemiah was sad; his heart was broken for his people and city. He determined to take action. He was willing to risk his job, his way of life, and even his physical safety in order to change the plight of his people.

Often situations that break our hearts will define our purpose. Bill Hybels, pastor of Willow Creek Church, calls it the Popeye Principle. Hybels observes that great leaders resemble the cartoon character

Popeye. For example: Popeye courts his girlfriend, Olive Oyl. His nemesis, Bluto, shows up, begins to beat Popeye up, and then eventually does something dastardly to Olive Oyl, like tie her to a train track. Just when it appears all hope is lost, Popeye says, "I've had all I can stands; I can't stands no more!"

That's what great leaders have in common: a moment when action must take over. So it was with Nehemiah.

Vince Lombardi said, "In life, many things will grab your eyes, but only a few will grab your heart. Pursue those." Good advice, don't you think? So, what is God putting in your heart? Keep your eyes open; it just might be the purpose you've been looking for. Enjoy.

What do I want to say to God today?

What is God saying to me today?

WHAT IF I BLOW IT?
SIN

Read 1 John 2:1-6.

What happens if I fail? This is a common question most of us will ask at some point in our journey. The truth is we all experience failure at one time or another. It is helpful to remember the same God who delivered us from the acts of sin we've committed does not abandon us when there's a problem.

Let's suppose you live in Los Angeles and you want to drive across the country to New York City. Even though you check your car to see if it is reliable, fill up with gas, and get up-to-date directions, it is entirely possible at some point in the journey you may have a problem. So what do you do?

1. Ignore the problem and hope it goes away.
2. Pull over; assess the problem; fix the problem; continue the journey.
3. Pull over; assess the problem; decide the problem is too dangerous; head back to Los Angeles.

I highly recommend choice #2. The same is true of our journey with Jesus. When we discover there's a problem, we need to recognize it for what it is. Nothing less; nothing more. We need to acknowledge it as sin, confess, repent, and get back on the road. To deny there's a problem—that we've sinned—will only make the problem worse. But to give up and turn back because we have a problem doesn't acknowledge Jesus is with us and that He is able to help us overcome the problem. In this world, challenges come with every path. Isn't it better to be traveling somewhere worthwhile than to return to a path we know brought us failure and pain?

This Scripture passage gives us some important advice. Let's look at some important truths about sin in this passage.

- We don't have to sin (1 John 2:1).
- But we might sin (1 John 1:2:1).
- If we do sin, it doesn't have to end the journey. God has a solution (1 John 2:1).
- It is wrong to go around sinning and acting like it doesn't matter; we are wrong (1 John 2:3-5).

So, if you have a problem, fix it. If, in the process of fixing the problem, the Mechanic says you've been driving too fast, or accelerating too quickly, listen and adjust. There's no need to keep making the same mistakes over and over again. The ultimate defense against sin is a personal and deep relationship with Christ. Travel with Jesus and He will lead you away from sin. Stay in His Word, and the sin in your life will not go undetected. Your Mechanic is on the job (Hebrews 7:25). Trust Him. Enjoy, but watch your speed.

What do I want to say to God today?

What is God saying to me today?

THE HOLY SPIRIT

Read John 14:15-26 and 16:5-15.

In these passages, Jesus is preparing His disciples for His physical absence. Jesus knows that if His followers are to truly experience His power in their lives, He must be *in* them. Enter the Holy Spirit. The Spirit has been involved in lives up to this point, but is about to do an even greater work within every Christian. Salvation and sanctification are inside jobs.

The Holy Spirit has been called the "Hound of Heaven" because He is the pursuing voice of God calling everyone to repentance. He is the voice of God speaking righteousness into a taunted and dirty world. He is a Counselor, a Comforter, a Guide, and an amazing Gift. The Holy Spirit sometimes moves with great and mighty power and at other times He speaks in a gentle whisper. He produces the fruit of "love, joy, peace, patience, kindness, goodness, faithfulness, gentleness and self-control" (Galatians 5:22) in our lives. He reminds us of the words of Christ and intercedes for us in prayer when we don't know how to pray.

In a way the Holy Spirit is also our personal GPS who uses the Word of God to guide us away from trouble and into the will of God. We are called to "live by the Spirit" (Romans 8). Such living keeps us spiritually safe, pure, and sanctified or set aside for God's use (Romans 15:16). Remember that the Holy Spirit will only speak what is consistent with what God has spoken through the Scriptures. That's why the Word of God is so important in our lives.

Welcome the presence of the Holy Spirit. Listen for His voice. Watch for His guidance. And be comforted by His grace. Enjoy.

What do I want to say to God today?

What is God saying to me today?

SANCTIFICATION

Farther along with Jesus than you ever dreamed possible.

Read Romans 7:21-8:4 and 1 Thessalonians 5:23-24.

Every person has a two-fold sin problem. First, there are the acts of sin he or she commits. Christ died on the cross for these so we might be forgiven. When you prayed to receive Christ, the Father, Son, and Holy Spirit forgave your sin, took up residence in your life, and began to initiate change. But there's another problem, and that is the nature of sin that lives inside every person.

Often called the "old man," inbred sin, carnality, the law of sin, double-mindedness, depraved nature, or root of bitterness, the sinful nature is humanity's problem because we are born with it. It is that desire to want things our way; putting ourselves first; and pushing God and others out.

After we're saved, the struggle ensues between God living in us, and the sinful nature (Romans 6, 7, 8). It's like a mutiny on a ship. The apostle Paul refers to it as causing him to do things he hates and not do the things he wants to do. It creates an up and down spiritual rollercoaster ride. Paul laments he is a "prisoner of the law of sin at work within my members. What a wretched man I am! Who will rescue me from this body of death?" (Romans 7:23-24).

The "body of death" illustration is a picture of Roman justice. Often Roman judges would prescribe the death penalty upon someone by sentencing him to be chained to a dead body until the infection caused by the decaying flesh began to destroy them. It was a horrible, slow, terrible way to die, and certainly no way to live! The apostle Paul equates wrestling with sin with being chained to that dead body.

Think about it. The bent towards selfishness goes with them everywhere. Selfishness enters every relationship. Self-centeredness pollutes every action. They take it to work. They drag it into their families. They cannot leave it even if they want to. I am so glad Paul doesn't stop there. He asks a very important question. "Who will rescue me from this body of death?" He provides an even more important answer: "Thanks be to God—through Jesus Christ our Lord!" (Romans 7:25).

If you have reached a place in your journey where you are struggling with the difference between what you want to be and who you truly are, the Holy Spirit will set you free! Don't be discouraged; even the disciples struggled, arguing about who would get to sit on the right and left hand of Jesus. In the garden of Gethsemane, their courage failed, and they abandoned Jesus.

Look at the difference between the disciples before they were sanctified at Pentecost. They were afraid and uncertain, vacillating in their commitment to Jesus. Afterwards they lived in the power and joy of the Holy Spirit just like Jesus promised they would (Acts 1:4).

We experience our own Pentecost or sanctification in much the same way the disciples did. Our sanctification comes when we want all of God and we give Him all of us. Sanctification, like our salvation, is a gift of God's grace. It is provided by the blood of Jesus and worked in us through the power of the Holy Spirit. Yield to Him, and He will sanctify you. Ask God to sanctify you, and He will be faithful to do it. God wants you to enjoy the journey.

What do I want to say to God today?

What is God saying to me today?

TEMPTATION

Read 1 Corinthians 10:13, Hebrews 4:15, and James 1:2-4.

Temptation is natural, or common to everyone (1 Corinthians 10:13). Temptation doesn't happen because you're bad; it happens because you're human. It is important to remember when making choices about how you are going to live, there are some roads a Christian just shouldn't walk down anymore.

Temptation is neutral; it is not the same as sin (Hebrews 4:15).

Just because you are tempted does not mean that you have sinned. Jesus was tempted and did not sin.

Temptation is necessary for growth (James 1:2-4). God allows us to be tempted because it reveals weaknesses that we need to address.

Webster describes temptation as "to tempt or entice to do something wrong." One thing for sure, the enemy never gives up attempting to deceive us. He will change his tactics over time, but there will always be issues of temptation for us to deal with.

I have some friends who came to Christ after they had been living together for a couple of years. Shortly after being saved, they realized their living arrangements needed to change. There were children involved, and the marriage date was a few months off. They determined to stay in the same house but change the sleeping arrangements so they would not be tempted to have sexual relations. They asked me what I thought. All I could do was say, "Good luck with that."

They were at the altar four Sundays straight before he moved back into his parents' house until their marriage. Their choice to obey God and stay pure until marriage served as a wonderful example to the children of what it means to honor God.

The Bible does not promise we won't be tempted. However, it does promise us a way of escape; a Friend who knows and understands; and victory if we hang in there. Enjoy.

TEMPTATION

What do I want to say to God today?

What is God saying to me today?

JESUS AND TEMPTATION

Read Matthew 4:1-11.

Even Jesus was tempted. That should make you feel better. Let's look at how Jesus handled temptation; it will serve as an important part of learning how to handle our own temptation.

Jesus was "led by the Spirit into the desert to be tempted by the devil" (Matthew 4:1-2). Notice it was the Spirit who led Jesus into the desert, but it was the devil that tempted Him. God does not tempt us. He will, however, allow us to be tempted.

Jesus was tempted at a time when He was physically and emotionally weak. I have learned to take extra precaution when I am sick, tired, or both. It is in these moments it seems we are most vulnerable to temptation. And be sure the enemy knows that.

Jesus answered temptation with Scripture. It is the Word of God that helps us in times of difficulty. Read it. Meditate on it. Memorize it.

Does it surprise you Satan answered back with Scripture? This should be a reminder that we need to study, search, and know God's Word. The enemy will incorrectly use, twist, and pervert it in an attempt to defeat us. A friend used to remind me, "You don't have to memorize Scripture, but remember the enemy has."

Temptation only lasts so long at a time. Do not be discouraged. Hang on to God. The Lord will always provide a way of escape from whatever it is the enemy throws at you, and you will come through stronger for the battle.

The enemy will be back at "an opportune time" (Luke 4:13). You can be sure the enemy will return. We are never beyond temptation. Christians need to be aware of and alert for attacks from the enemy.

Christians do not have to live in fear of Satan. When Jesus redeems us, we are totally redeemed. However, you do need to remember you're not home yet. There's a word for people who think they are beyond temptation: victims. Don't be one. Enjoy.

What do I want to say to God today?

What is God saying to me today?

THE 23RD PSALM *VERSES 1-3*

Read Psalm 23.

There is probably no more recognizable passage of Scripture than the 23rd Psalm. It has been the subject of countless books, songs, and works of art. I once read of a psychiatrist who so believed in the power of this text that he prescribed it to an anxiety-ridden executive three times a day. He literally took out a pad of paper and wrote the following prescription: "The 23rd Psalm is to be read as follows: once in the morning, once at noon, and once before bed, for a period of 30 days."

The executive found what many have found—the 23rd Psalm is powerful. As you read it today, let me challenge you to do so in an unhurried manner and to consider each line.

"The Lord is my shepherd." You may be a sheep, but you're not without a Shepherd. Yours is the finest Shepherd a sheep ever knew.

"I shall not be in want." The Shepherd provides for his sheep 100 percent of the time. He will take care of you. What are your needs today? The Shepherd knows. The Shepherd will provide.

"He makes me lie down in green pastures." Sometimes we have to be forced to rest. Your Shepherd will do that; you can trust whatever rest He calls you to. The pastures of your rest will be rich and green. If things aren't happening as fast you'd like, perhaps He wants you to have some downtime.

"He leads me beside quiet waters." It is said that sheep are skittish, not even willing to drink from water that is not still. He knows how to get you to a place where it is safe to drink. What are you afraid of today?

"He restores my soul." Sometimes the fleece of a sheep can become so matted with mud and heavy with wool that once toppled, they cannot get up again. They will literally suffocate from the weight of their own matted fleece if the shepherd does not right them. What do you need to share with your Shepherd?

"He guides me in paths of righteousness for his name's sake." Our Shepherd, Jesus, always leads and guides. He will do so, not only because He loves us, but because we are His. His Name is at stake.

In heaven we will be able to look back over our lives and realize that Jesus never failed us. Not even once. Every decision He made was true. Even when His will momentarily causes us pain, we will look back and see what He did was right for us at the time. Jesus never fails. Note the number of times "he" is used in this psalm. Consider the absolute trust that David has in the Shepherd.

Sometimes we need to set aside time to marvel at just how far the Shepherd will go to care for us. These verses are the words of a shepherd who spent his days and nights caring for his sheep. And then one day he looked at the sheep and realized that what he was to the sheep, God had been to him. You have a wonderful Shepherd. Enjoy His presence.

What do I want to say to God today?

What is God saying to me today?

THE 23RD PSALM *VERSES 4-6*

Read Psalm 23.

A well-known childhood prayer starts like this, "Now I lay me down to sleep, I pray the Lord my soul to keep." I recently heard a comedian say the prayer was fine up to this point, but then it takes a strange twist—"If I should die before I wake, I pray the Lord my soul to take." The comedian's comment was at that moment both of his eyes came open. "Who said anything about dying?" The childhood prayer designed to comfort a child before bed, suddenly brought fear. That's a little how the 23rd Psalm feels when you get to verse 4.

"Even though I walk through the valley of the shadow of death." The harsh reality is we all have to walk through dangerous valleys in our lives; the good news here is the word "through." With Jesus as our Shepherd, the valley is not our destination, but the route we travel to make it home. This phrase also speaks to the maturity of our faith. It is one thing to trust a God who will never ask us to walk through dark valleys or who will protect us from them; it is quite another to trust in spite of where the pathway leads.

"I will fear no evil, for you are with me." It is the presence of God that gives comfort and peace in the valley. This presence is real. This presence is powerful. This presence is promised to His sheep.

"Your rod and your staff, they comfort me." In *A Shepherd Looks at the 23rd Psalm*, Philip Keller notes the peace the sheep feel, due in large part to the tools the presence of the shepherd carries. Jesus came out of the grave with the keys to death and the grave.

"You prepare a table before me in the presence of my enemies." It is one thing for a table to be prepared for us in the absence of enemies, but our Shepherd has the ability to prepare His table for us in the presence of our enemies. Whatever your enemy is today, Jesus will still prepare His table for you. Nowhere have we seen this more true than in the lives of our soldiers who have found an amazing peace in the midst of very difficult days because of God's ability to prepare His table in the presence of our enemies.

"You anoint my head with oil." The shepherd used oil to rub on the head of the sheep for a couple different reasons. First, the oil would medicate any wounds left by insect or thorns. Secondly, the oil served as a lubricant when the sheep butted heads, as sheep are often known to do, so they would glance off of each other and not do permanent damage to one another. The applications for this are obvious.

"My cup overflows." God's goodness is never measured. His blessings always exceed expectations.

"Surely goodness and mercy shall follow me all the days of my life" (NKJV). "Goodness and mercy are like guard dogs for the Christian," I heard one old-time evangelist say. "They will follow you everywhere you go."

"And I will dwell in the house of the Lord forever." No more roaming. No more wandering. This sheep has found a home.

Enjoy.

What do I want to say to God today?

What is God saying to me today?

FAITH

Read Mark 9:14-27, Romans 10:17, and Hebrews 11:1.

I used to think that having faith meant I would say I believed something even if I truly didn't, like the Chicago Cubs were going to win the World Series. Well, I was wrong about faith and the Cubs.

Then I thought if I just tried really hard, I could make myself believe something I didn't truly believe to begin with. Well, I was wrong and confused.

The world is full of wrong and confused messages about faith. That's why it's important to go to the Word of God for the answer. Faith is not pretending or trying really hard to believe something you don't believe. Faith is being sure and certain that something God has said is true and then being willing to live like it (Hebrews 11:1).

One of the things I love about following Jesus is I don't have to pretend. I can be who I am when I'm with Jesus. As a matter of fact, He prefers me that way.

Notice the words of the father to Jesus in this story. Especially the words in Mark 9:24: "I do believe; help me overcome my unbelief!"

Jesus, who had been teaching his disciples about faith and belief in him, gives them a living example of what it means. A father comes to him with a possessed son tortured by convulsions. The father is struggling with his faith because Jesus' disciples were unable to do anything for the boy. The father's uncertainty is made clear in his honest words to Jesus, "If you can do anything." He didn't pretend with Jesus, he was honest. Jesus, in return, honored the man's diminished faith and healed his son. I believe the father's faith in Jesus grew from that point on, don't you?

What are you struggling with today? Do you have enough faith to bring your struggles to God? You don't have to pretend to know the outcome, just have faith enough to bring your troubles to God. He will take care of the rest. Remember, it is not the amount of faith, but to whom you go with your faith, that makes all the difference.

If you would like to learn more about faith, look at these additional verses: Hebrews 11, James 2:26, and James 5:13-20. They will help you enjoy the journey. Enjoy!

FAITH

What do I want to say to God today?

What is God saying to me today?

PRAYER

Read Luke 11:1-4 and Acts 12:1-18.

The disciples only ever asked Jesus to teach them how to do one thing. There could have been a lot of things, but there was only one. It wasn't how to walk on water, how to raise the dead, how to turn water into wine, or even how to make a difference in the world. The disciples asked Jesus to teach them how to pray. Most writers suggest the reason they asked that was because they knew the secret to everything else He did was His ability to talk directly with the Father. It's still true to this day. Prayer is the key that unlocks heaven's door.

Prayer is a learned behavior. It is not something secret or mysterious. There are no special rites that proceeded Jesus' prayers. He is happy to teach them to pray. Notice when Jesus teaches them it is not a long prayer, nor a flowery or loud prayer, but an honest, sincere, and humble prayer. That kind of prayer is powerful. Let's consider Peter's situation.

Peter was in jail, locked behind prison walls. The people who loved him couldn't do anything physically to help him. They weren't powerful enough to overthrow the Romans and take the prison by force. They weren't influential enough to secure his release through diplomatic means. They were almost helpless. I said almost. What they could do was pray; and they did.

I am amazed at the number of times when I do what I can and God fills in the rest.

"So Peter was kept in prison, but the church was earnestly praying to God for him" (Acts 12:5).

The difference in Peter's life was the prayers of God's people. So what do we learn from these two passages?

- Prayer is talking with God. It is honest, earnest, and humble communication between God's child, you, and Him. You do not have to use some special "churchy" language—just talk to God.
- We are invited into the very presence of God; we have been gifted the privilege of communing with our "Father."
- We are invited to share our words of honor, praise, and thanks to our Father.
- Through prayer, we surrender ourselves to God the Father as we seek His will for our lives.
- We are invited to bring our concerns and needs to our Father.
- It is through prayer we confess our sins and ask forgiveness.
- Through prayer we intercede and pray for others.
- The prayers of Christians are powerful and make a difference.

Some additional Scriptures for reading and studying: Luke 18:1-8, Philippians 4:6-7, 1 Thessalonians 5:17, James 5:16.

Your prayers, prayed humbly and earnestly before God, are vital to your relationship with the Father. Have you talked to your Father today? He's waiting. Enjoy the journey.

What do I want to say to God today?

What is God saying to me today?

HOW DO I KNOW GOD IS TALKING TO ME?

Read John 10:1-5 and 14:24.

The key to effective prayer is talking *with* God and not just *at* Him. Sometimes we have a tendency to talk *at* God. In other words, we talk but never listen. We sometimes treat prayer as if we're pulling up and ordering from a fast food restaurant. We place our order, pick it up, and then go on our way—the faster the better.

So then, how do we do the listening part of prayer? How do we know it is God talking to us? Does God speak audibly? What does He sound like? How do we know it's not just our imagination?

God speaks through many venues: our conscience and thoughts, music, Christian friends, Christian literature and poetry, nature, preaching and teaching, and on and on. You can be sure, though, that God always speaks through His Word. Listening to God is best done as we read His Word. Through God's Word the Holy Spirit teaches, encourages, admonishes, empowers, and guides us. I've never heard God speak audibly, but I have discovered His guidance as I prayed and spent time reading the Bible. Verses seem to jump out of Scripture. Those moments were not audible moments, but they were no less real. Let's look at some more important ideas about communication with God.

Learning to recognize God's voice and differentiate it from the plethora of other issues and voices calling to us is a matter of practice.

I remember a particular football game I played in high school. My father was a child of the Depression who strongly valued work and who never truly understood the attraction of games. He only came to one of my football games that year. I was a defensive lineman. On one particular play, I slipped past the center and got a hand on the quarterback just as he was passing the ball. The quarterback went down and the ball was deflected up into the air where one of our linebackers grabbed it and ran for a touchdown. The dust settled, and I looked downfield and watched our linebacker score. Then it happened. I heard his voice; my father's. I can still hear it to this day. I heard it above the cheers of the crowd and the directions of the coaches and the whistle of the referee. My father yelled three simple words that day I will remember forever. I knew his voice. I'd heard it call me from bed to breakfast every morning. I'd heard it across a room when I needed to tone things down a bit. I'd heard it when he was doing something around the house and needed a hand. I'd heard it when it was time to leave for church or come in from playing. I'd heard it when he responded to my call: "Dad? Where are you?" So on that Saturday morning, it was not difficult for me to pick his voice out of the crowd. When William Wangler yelled, "That's my boy!" his son heard him, and still hears him to this day. That's the power of the voice of a father speaking to his son.

Do you recognize your heavenly Father's voice? He is speaking to you, personally, lovingly, and consistently. As you continue to journey with Him, listen to Him, talk to Him, and answer Him, be assured you will begin to recognize His voice. He is with you and He is not silent. You will learn to recognize his voice if you spend time with Him. Enjoy this time!

What do I want to say to God today?

What is God saying to me today?

DO WHATEVER HE TELLS YOU TO DO

Read John 2:1-11.

I wonder what the disciples thought when they discovered their first road trip with Jesus was to a wedding banquet? That probably wasn't what they were expecting. That's the thing about following Jesus—He often takes us where we least expect to go.

There is a statement in this story I hope you will remember as you continue on your journey. Sometime after arriving, Mary the mother of Jesus approached Him, "They have no more wine."

"Dear woman, why do you involve me? My time has not yet come," Jesus gently rebuffed.

Apparently, Mary thought it was Jesus' time to shine. I don't know how much time elapsed, but she next said, "Do whatever He tells you to do." The result was a miracle and water was turned into wine.

Just after becoming a Christian I lost my job. The situation was dire. I called my parents and asked them to pray. They assured me they would and my mother added, "Son, your whole life you have lived by your gut and it's got you into nothing but trouble. It's because Jesus wasn't living in you. But you're different now. I want you to listen because He is going to lead you. Stay in the Word and stay on your knees. Look and listen for His leading and then do whatever He tells you to do."

Two days later I accepted a position in my brother's business working on a garbage truck, a job that would provide for my family for the next three years.

A few weeks later I registered at the local community college because I felt God wanted me to. I took the first class that was available but had no idea what I was supposed to study. I also didn't have the money for tuition. I sought my pastor's counsel. He explained one could attend up to three sessions before payment was required and that he had a hunch God would provide.

I registered and went to the first class without even a book. Apparently they wanted money for those. During class, the instructor walked over and dropped a used copy on my desk. He said I could use one of his until I purchased one.

By the third class session, I knew this is where I needed to be, but still did not have the money for books or tuition, and the financial situation at home was dismal. Discouraged, I went to class anyway. At the end of the session, I picked up my belongings and walked to Mr. Berry's desk to return the loaned book. He was talking with a student so I laid the book on the edge of his desk and turned to walk out. "Brian, can you hang around for a second? I need to talk with you," said Mr. Berry.

When the other student left, Mr. Berry turned to me, "Brian, this teaching job is just a part-time position for me. My full time job is administering a program for the State of Illinois Department of Children and Family Services. I manage a group of social workers that helps kids. One of the tools we use is a court-appointed advocate who spends two to four hours a week with these kids. We pay a little more than minimum wage, cover all mileage and entertainment expenses, and you can create your own schedule. It's not easy work, but I've been watching you and have a hunch you would be great for this position. Are you interested?"

Trying not to sound too excited, I said, "Yes, I am."

As we left the room, Mr. Berry added, "Oh, and by the way. As long as you work for me, all of your tuition and books are paid for by the State of Illinois."

As I stood there amazed, I could hear my mother say, "Do whatever He tells you to do." Enjoy the journey. I am.

What do I want to say to God today?

What is God saying to me today?

I pray you have enjoyed these thirty-one days of devotions. Please know it has been an honor to share a small part of this journey with you. Some of the subjects we've discussed are deep and difficult. You may have many more questions today than you did when you started and that's okay. We have only scratched the surface with regard to who God is and how He works. You have the rest of your life to work out your relationship with God and all He has for you. The characters we've met in Scripture are timeless and powerful. The God we've been learning to listen to is faithful. Enjoy!

CONTACT INFORMATION

For bulk order discounts of this book or additional resources, please visit the author's website:

BrianWangler.com

To order additional copies of this book, please visit
www.redemption-press.com.
Also available on Amazon.com and BarnesandNoble.com
Or by calling toll free 1-844-2REDEEM.

CPSIA information can be obtained
at www.ICGtesting.com
Printed in the USA
FFOW03n2039290318
46047914-46954FF